Peaches All the Time

by Margie Burton, Cathy French, and Tammy Jones

Table of Contents

Can I Eat Peaches All the Time?

I like to eat peaches.

The peach juice drips down my chin when
I take big bites.

My mom will not buy peaches all the time. Sometimes they cost too much money.

Why do peaches cost
too much money sometimes?

How Do Peaches Grow?

Peaches grow on trees.
They are picked in the summer.

We grow lots of peaches. The state of Georgia grows so many peaches that its nickname is the Peach State.

Peaches need water to grow.
Sometimes the rain gives the trees
all the water they need.

How Do Peaches Get Water When There Is Not Much Rain?

Sometimes there is not much rain. We must water the trees to help the peaches grow.

Pipes bring water to the trees. This is called irrigation.

When the peaches grow well, farmers can send many of them to the stores.

The more peaches there are for sale, the less they cost.

How Do Peaches Grow When There Is Too Much Rain?

Sometimes it rains too much.
Too much water is bad for the peaches.

The peaches go bad when they get too much water.

We give the bad peaches to the animals.

The farmers cannot sell the bad peaches. They do not have very many good ones to send to the stores.

The fewer peaches there are for sale,
the more the peaches cost.

Now I know why my mom
will not buy peaches all the time.

The weather can make a big
difference in the price of peaches.